SCATALOG
A Kid's Field Guide to Animal Poop

HOW TO TRACK A HYENA

Henry Owens

"BECAUSE EVERYBODY POOPS"

WINDMILL
BOOKS
New York

Published in 2014 by Windmill Books, An Imprint of Rosen Publishing
29 East 21st Street, New York, NY 10010

First Edition

Editor: Amelie von Zumbusch
Photo Research: Katie Stryker
Book Design: Colleen Bialecki

Photo Credits: Cover (top) Anup Shah/The Image Bank/Getty Images; cover (bottom) Anthony Bannister/Gallo Images/Getty Images; background Gary Ombler/Dorling Kindersley/Getty Images; pp. 4, 9 iStock/Thinkstock; p. 5 Diana/Flickr; p. 6 Elliot Neep/Oxford Scientific/Getty Images; pp. 8, 16 Gualtiero Boffi/Shutterstock.com; p. 11 Bridgena Barnard/Shutterstock.com; p. 12 David Lazar/Flickr Open/Getty Images; p. 13 Datacaft Co Ltd/Getty Images; p. 15 Dave Pusey/Shutterstock.com; p. 17 (top left) Mogens Trolle/Shutterstock.com; p. 17 (top right) Javarman/Shutterstock.com; p. 17 (bottom left) Andrew Molinaro/Shutterstock.com; p. 17 (bottom right) Albie Venter/Shutterstock.com; p. 19 Sam Thorton/Flickr; p. 20 Beverly Joubert/National Geographic/Getty Images; p. 21 Daryl Balfour/Gallo Images/Getty Images; p. 22 Gerald Hinde/Gallo Images/Getty Images.

Library of Congress Cataloging-in-Publication Data

Owens, Henry.
How to track a hyena / by Henry Owens. — First edition.
    pages cm. — (Scatalog: a kid's field guide to animal poop)
Includes index.
ISBN 978-1-61533-889-4 (library) — ISBN 978-1-61533-895-5 (pbk.) —
ISBN 978-1-61533-901-3 (6-pack)
1. Hyenas—Juvenile literature. 2. Animal droppings—Juvenile literature. I. Title.
QL737.C24O94 2014
599.74'3—dc23
                              2013030207

Manufactured in the United States of America

CPSIA Compliance Information: Batch #BW14WM: For Further Information contact Windmill Books, New York, New York at 1-866-478-0556

CONTENTS

Have you ever heard an animal laugh? Spotted hyenas are famous for their laughing noises. They make these excited sounds when they find food. There are three types of hyenas, including striped hyenas and brown hyenas. Spotted hyenas are the largest and most common type of hyena.

In the past, people misunderstood hyenas. For example, hyenas were once associated with witches. Tracking hyenas helps us understand how hyenas really act.

Here, a tracker examines some hyena poop. After it dries, hyena poop forms dry, chalky clumps.

If you wanted to track, or find, a spotted hyena in the wild, you could listen for the sound of its laugh. An easier way to track animals, though, is by looking on the ground for their poop! If you spot hyena poop, you will know a hyena has passed by.

5

WHERE TO FIND HYENAS

If you wanted to track spotted hyenas, you would have to visit Africa. That is where all wild spotted hyenas live. Hyenas live in a wide range of African **habitats**. They can be found in forests, mountains, deserts, and **savannas**. A savanna is a grassland with few trees or bushes.

National parks are a good place to track hyenas. This hyena is chasing flamingos in Kenya's Lake Nakuru National Park.

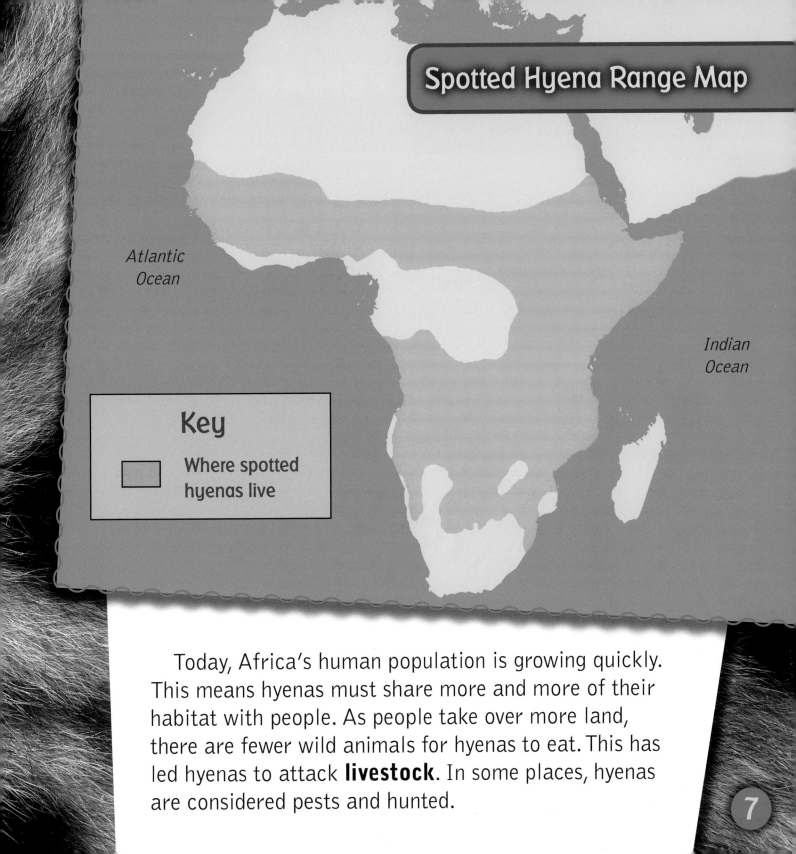

Spotted Hyena Range Map

Atlantic Ocean

Indian Ocean

Key

Where spotted hyenas live

Today, Africa's human population is growing quickly. This means hyenas must share more and more of their habitat with people. As people take over more land, there are fewer wild animals for hyenas to eat. This has led hyenas to attack **livestock**. In some places, hyenas are considered pests and hunted.

7

RECOGNIZING HYENAS

When you look at a spotted hyena, you may think it looks a little like a dog. However, hyenas are more closely related to cats. Unlike in many animal **species**, female spotted hyenas are actually bigger than males. Other than that, males and females look a lot alike. Even experienced trackers have trouble telling them apart by sight.

Spotted hyenas can measure up to 35 inches (89 cm) tall. They weigh between 90 and 190 pounds (41–86 kg).

Hyenas can eat a lot very quickly. This is because they have very acidic juices in their stomachs, which let their bodies break down food very quickly.

Spotted hyenas have strong bodies. Their powerful jaws and teeth allow them to rip through the meat, bones, and hooves of the animals they eat. Hyenas also have large hearts. This helps them run at great speeds over long distances without getting tired.

Hyenas are social animals. They live together in large groups, called clans. The clan is led by a female hyena. Other females and their cubs are **ranked** below the leader. At the lowest rank are the males. High-ranking females and their cubs get to eat first and cool off in the best mud baths.

Hyenas often use sounds to **communicate** with others in their clan. Hyenas make squeals, groans, and other noises to call for help and to tell cubs to come back to their mothers. Hyenas can hear each other's laughs from 3 miles (5 km) away. Hyena sounds help trackers find hyenas, too.

A spotted hyena clan can have as many as 80, or sometimes even 100, members. The clan's females are more aggressive, or likely to fight, than its males are.

Each spotted hyena clan has its own **territory**. A territory is land where an animal or group of animals lives and finds its food. Near the center of the hyenas' territory is their underground den. Clan members work together to defend their territory from intruders.

Hyenas are very aggressive, both with members of their own clan and outsiders. They can be dangerous to people.

12

These clan members are gathered around the clan den. The clan's cubs stay in the den, while adults use it as a central meeting area.

Spotted hyenas mark their territory with sticky goo from their scent **glands**. They also use poop to mark their land. They leave it around the territory in areas called **latrines**. These signs tell intruding hyenas that a certain clan already controls the area. Latrines also serve as clues for trackers, who know hyenas are nearby if they spot one.

HYENA CUBS

If trackers are lucky, they might spot hyena cubs. Female hyenas give birth to one to four cubs at a time. The cubs are born with black hair and sharp teeth. For the first few weeks, cubs live with their mother in a separate den away from the rest of the clan.

When they are three or four weeks old, the cubs move into the clan den with other cubs from the clan. Hyena cubs fight with each other to see which will have a higher rank. At about two years old, male cubs will leave the territory and find a new clan to join.

The best way to catch a glimpse of a hyena cub is to figure out where either the clan's den is or a mother's den for her newborns is.

Hyenas are known as **scavengers**. Scavengers are animals that eat dead animals that they find. However, spotted hyenas actually hunt for most of the food they eat. Hyenas hunt antelope, zebras, and even rhinoceroses! They will also eat birds, snakes, and insects.

Spotted hyenas use sight, hearing, and smell to sense both prey and carrion, or dead animals. They tend to scavenge during the day and hunt at night.

16

RECOGNIZING SIGNS OF KILLS BY DIFFERENT PREDATORS

African Wild Dog
- Remains scattered near kill site
- Stomach usually eaten
- Bones scattered or eaten

Leopard
- Kill often dragged away
- Stomach left or buried
- Long bones unbroken

Spotted Hyena
- Remains left at kill site
- Stomach partly eaten
- Bones crushed or eaten

Hyenas often hunt in groups of two to five. Sometimes one hyena will distract a herd of animals while another hyena catches a young or sick member of that herd. Even when hyenas work together, higher-ranked hyenas always eat first! Hyena kills are messy. Trackers recognize hyena kills by the scattered fur they leave and other signs.

ALL ABOUT POOP

Hyenas **digest** nearly all parts of the animals they eat, including skin, teeth, and bone. Animal bones contain a lot of a **mineral** called calcium. This calcium comes out in hyenas' poop. As the poop dries in the sun, the calcium makes it turn white!

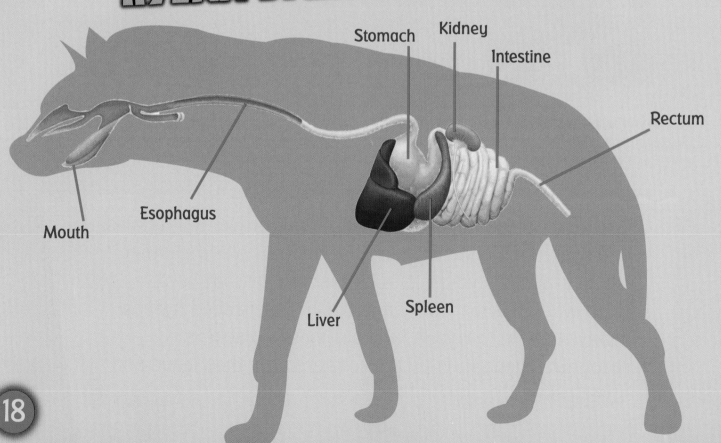

HYENA DIGESTIVE SYSTEM

Stomach

Kidney

Intestine

Rectum

Esophagus

Mouth

Liver

Spleen

Hairs

White

Segments

Hyena poop has segments, or joined parts. Fresh poop may look green or brown, but it will turn very white as it dries.

HYENA POOP

One of the only parts of an animal that a hyena does not digest is hair. The hair passes through the hyena and comes out in its poop. Scientists have found human hairs in **fossilized** hyena poop that is over 200,000 years old! These hairs may be able to tell scientists more about how humans developed.

HYENA TRACKING TIPS

Hyena poop looks very different from the poop of most other animals. This makes it a great way to track hyenas. Safari guides also look for footprints to see if hyenas have been in an area. Hyena footprints are large and easy to recognize. Trackers also look for the sticky goo hyenas leave on trees and grasses.

Four toes

Side toes curved

Claw marks

HYENA TRACKS

Some scientists study hyenas by putting radio collars on them. The collars let the scientists track the hyenas' movements and learn more about their habits.

Instead of tracking hyenas, some scientists get hyenas to come to them. They do this by playing the sounds of hyena calls. Hyenas can recognize the calls of other clan members. If they think a hyena in their clan is in trouble, they will often come to help out.

In some parts of Africa, people often kill hyenas. In other areas, hyenas and people live together peacefully. In northern Ethiopia, hyenas help farmers by eating dead livestock. This also gives the hyenas an easy way to find food.

In the past, many people feared and hated hyenas. Hopefully, trackers can help us learn to understand and respect these smart animals. After all, humans and hyenas will likely be sharing more land in the future.

Spotted hyenas are unusual in many ways, including their white poop and their female-led clans. Much of what we know about them is thanks to trackers.

GLOSSARY

communicate (kuh-MYOO-nih-kayt) To share facts or feelings.

digest (dy-JEST) To break down food so that the body can use it.

fossilized (FO-suh-lyzd) Hardened and preserved, or kept safe.

glands (GLANDZ) Parts of the body that produce an element to help with a bodily function.

habitats (HA-buh-tats) The kinds of land where an animal or a plant naturally lives.

latrines (luh-TREENZ) Places where animals or people leave their waste.

livestock (LYV-stok) Animals raised by people.

mineral (MIN-rul) Natural matter that is not an animal, a plant, or another living thing.

ranked (RANKD) Having a place above or below others in a group.

savannas (suh-VA-nuz) Grasslands with few trees or bushes.

scavengers (SKA-ven-jurz) Animals that eat dead things.

species (SPEE-sheez) One kind of living thing. All people are one species.

territory (TER-uh-tor-ee) Land or space that animals guard for their use.

INDEX

WEBSITES

For web resources related to the subject of this book, go to:
www.windmillbooks.com/weblinks and select this book's title.